Just Rhymes

A collection of poems

by

E. L. Sawyer
Creston Iowa

compiled by
Richard Gantt
(Rex Passion)

Published in Canada By Komatik Press

62 Lower St., Torbay, NL. A1K 1B3

www.komatikpress.com

rex1@rcn.com

LISBN (paperback) 987-0-9987113-5-5

ISBN (hardcover) 978-0-9828219-6-1

ISBN (eBook) 978-0-9987113-9-3

Book and cover design by Rex Passion

Komatik Press
Cambridge, St. John's

In Loving Memory

of

Sally-Jo Gantt Crabill

my dearest cousin and spiritual guide

March 4, 1947
April 22, 2015

Untitled Poem

Rewritten-clarity! Oh yeah! This is what Mom meant-I know it now.
You get to a certain age and your body time is spent.
Maybe well or not-you can seek it but it came and went.
Your bones ache and skin and muscles sag -
under each eye a "carry-on" bag...
...packed for out of town, outta here, gone, sacked.
My current color, shades of dead, gray hair, yellow freckled skin-
whose bag of bones did I crawl in?
I swear I am still only seventeen, twenty-four at most -
where did I go? Am I a ghost?
In my mind I'm still a child,
growing older, but ever wild.
Wow! A dream just called me, so I dialed.
Please hold me and listen-I feel defiled.
But-please hear-I am afraid
of growing ancient and not yet dead,
a thousand thoughts still in my head-.
..who cares tho-they're dumb and trite and over said.
Please don't forget about me.
Please say goodbye and smile at me, a kiss... (unfinished

Sally Gantt Crabill

Introduction

I grew up with stories about Grandpa Sawyer, but no living members of my family remember ever meeting him. But in 1993 my awareness of him changed when I received a comb-bound book from my Uncle Ab with the title *Just Rhymes* crudely hand-lettered on the cover. I quickly read a few of the sixty poems, then put the book aside and it languished on a shelf for two decades. When my cousin Sally passed away in the spring of 2015, I decided to bring his poems together in her, and his, memory.

Actually Eugene Lucas Sawyer, who was known to many as simply E. L., was not my "Grandpa," but rather my great- grandfather, my grandmother's father. He was born in 1874 in Creston, Iowa and later in life moved to Trenton, Missouri. His father, Henry P. Sawyer, was a railroad man who was buried with his conductor's hat atop his coffin and a lighted train lantern by its side. E. L. started out as a journalist but quickly became a trainman himself when he realized how little the newspaper business paid. At the age of thirty he lost his right arm in a railway accident and was paid the equivalent of nearly $40,000 for his injury. He went on to own a florist shop and a cab company in Creston for many years before the Depression.

E L. was both impressed and uncomfortable with the rapid pace of changing times. Zeppelins amazed him, as did the streamlined diesel train called the Zephyr, but he mourned the loss of the way things were in "the days gone by." His heroes were, among others, Charles Lindbergh, Thomas Edison, Will Rogers and Dizzy Dean. He was a hillbilly at heart, with a disdain for manners, grooming or money, much to his wife's chagrin. He had little time for people who were "too big for their britches," those who did not take voting seriously, or anyone who called him "Pap." He was disgusted by the public adoration of the bank robber, John Dillinger.

He was unimpressed by the benevolent intervention of God, except when he needed a new straw hat and freely dispensed advice: do a good deed every day, have a positive attitude, be yourself and keep your mouth shut.

He was sentimental about family, Iowa, fishing and springtime, and loved his two grandsons, one of whom was my father, very much. He was passionate about baseball on the radio and resigned to, afraid of, looking forward to and endlessly curious about his own death.

E. L. was an avid newspaper reader and an equally avid clipper. He cut out poems from, among others Grantland Rice, Abigail Cresson and the farmer-poet, Fred Lape. I can see the influence of these individuals in his work, which—because he was reluctant to call himself a poet—he referred to as "rhymes."

In many ways, E. L.'s poems offer a picture of life in the Midwest in the years between the wars. In the lines of his verse we learn about inventors, elections, the Depression, gangsters, death, fishing, and several World Series games. Poignantly we learn about his family and how important it was in his life.

Although most of the poems in this collection were typewritten, others come from a black-paged scrapbook with

7

words written in white ink, perhaps by E. L. himself, but perhaps not. "Casey Jones," "My Chauffeur," "What Then," and "1925 Series-Radio" are among those from the handwritten scrapbook.

In transcribing E. L.'s words I have kept his spelling, grammar and punctuation, whether right or wrong and the line spacing, whether or not it was actually his.

E. L.'s rhymes are not literary works, but rather a glimpse of a time now long gone. Through them, I have finally gotten to know my great-grandfather and have come to recognize parts of him not only in myself but in Sally as well. I am grateful for the opportunity to share these long-forgotten rhymes with you and in so doing, honor both my great-grandfather, E. L. and my dear cousin, Sally.

Richard Gantt (Rex Passion)
Cambridge, Massachusetts 2016

E L Sawyer

The poet's life is one sweet song
It lasts 'till some sweet day
Old death - The Reaper comes along
And chases him away.

My special thanks to David Agee Hoar who encouraged me repeatedly to publish E. L.'s Rhymes

The Zephyr — Burlington's New Motor Train

DIESEL POWERED
ELECTRICALLY CONTROLLED

A GLEAMING SHAFT OF STAINLESS STEEL

The Zepher

I went to see the train come in,
    As I did of yore;
But I was disappointed for –
    The train comes in no more.

No hissing steam nor clanging bell,
    No smoke arolling down;
No whistles screaming warnings,
    That woke up half the town.

No grease, no dirt, no anything
    Like in the days gone by;
I stood there like a dummy man –
    Could not believe my eye.

A silver shadow drifted past
    And stopped without a jar;
A beautiful, fantastic thing,
    You wonder where you are?

With wonderment and awe I gazed,
No dust nor any din;
Was I asleep or did I come
To see the train come in?

For there upon the track it stood,
A night club thing on wheels;
A panoramic night life scene
Before your eyes unreels.

And while I gazed in raptured bliss,
The phantom show moved on;
I forged ahead to see it go –
But lo, the thing was gone.

Just like a drifting summer breeze,
I knew not what it meant;
I went to see the train come in —
The Zepher came and went.

The Zeppelin

"The Zeppelin is coming." Great bird of the air,
Is there nothing that stops you, do you go everywhere?
You crossed the wide oceans and countries of snow,
Where mountains would baffle over you go.

The storms beat about you—would break you in two,
But lo and behold, you came safely through.
What staunchness there is, O bird without wings,
What power is let loose when your great motor sings;

How graceful you are on your trip in the sky,
As you rush sizzling past or hover close by.
Great craft of the air, uncovered are we,
When you pass overhead in rapt dignity.

Next

Columbus crossed the bloomin' ocean,
    Sailed upon its foamy crest;
People said the man was crazy,
    Columbus sailed and dik the rest.

Lindbergh flew the bonnie ocean,
    Flying high and very fast;
People said he'd never make it,
    Lindbergh did the job at last.

Sailing now upon its bosom,
    Flying high above its tide;
Maybe one will dive in under
    Crossing to the other side.

Changing times are always coming,
    Changing always for the best;
Striving men are all around us,
    Hoping now to beat the rest.

Thomas A. Edison

1847-1931

All bow to him, this super-man
    Who in a wizard's way,
Laughed at night and harnessed it,
    Then turned it into day.

New worlds he seeks to conquer,
    For here his work is done;
New hands will carry on for him
    A work so well begun.

What monument could e're be built
    That's suitable we say;
He left one here when he passed on,
    A monument for aye.

But now he's gone and we will lose,
    Not his light that gleams,
But he himself in draperies wrapped
    Lies down to pleasant dreams.

Now dim the light, for now he's dead,
    But don't grieve for him, but pray
That rest will come in his last sleep
    Forever and a day.

Lindbergh

A lonely boy, a crafty brain,
A single engine monoplane
A dream that proved both safe and sane-
 That's Lindbergh.

Without a care he hopped right in,
'Twas just like going on a spin,
With courage bold to make him win-
 That's Lindbergh.

A job to do, he did not shirk,
Nor did he even call it work,
Though dangers all about him lurk-
 That's Lindbergh.

While others waited weather fair,
He jumped right in for "over there,"
He only heard his mother's prayer-
 That's Lindbergh.

No pilot but his God had he,
To guide his craft across the sea,
To Paris or eternity-
 That's Lindbergh.

A hero made just over night,
A hero made for just one flight,
But he was sure that he was right-
    That's Lindbergh.

Such deeds have made this glorious land,
And always there were some on hand,
To meet the test when in demand-
    That's Lindbergh.

All Will Be Well

St. Peter listen to our plea;
Two souls took off today;
Please set your "beacon lights" aflame
To guide them on their way.

Two sturdy souls beloved by all
Their life work here is done;
Our hearts are sad, as they depart,
Towards the setting sun.

The world will mourn for Will and Post,
And we shall miss them here;
For they were staunch, courageous men
Who kept their records clear.

So when they land, turn "flood lights" on,
Your portals open wide;
And have your "ground crew" waiting there
For "three points down" inside.

And now on earth, they've done their "turn,"
See that they get their due;
St. Peter, harken to our prayer,
The rest we leave with you.

A Cocoanut

Way down in Cocoa, Florida,
    Where men, it seems do things;
A man has built an aeroplane,
    That really flaps its wings.

The wings have feathers like a bird,
    To help out in the flight;
He says they are essential,
    And I believe he's right.

It takes us back in history
    To one Darius Green,
Who built a plane that flapped its wings,
    The first one ever seen.

But times have changed, and Green is dead,
    Yet evolution brings;
A plane that flies, just like a bird
    That squawks and flaps its wings.

The plane will be equipped with brains,
    To be of any use;
Let's hope they use most any kind,
    Except those of a goose.

You ask "What flaps the wings," I know,
    "A flapper," then, says he;
A flapper flaps the wings and flies
    Far across the sea.

O, shades of Lindbergh, Chamberlin,
    Byrd and all the rest;
You've done your bit, you're far behind,
    But you have done your best.

We'll watch this "Bird of Paradise,"
    Bound for eternity;
For what she does and how she "flaps"
    Will soon be history.

Votah, Watch Yore Vote

'lection time am almost heah,
    Votah, watch yore vote;

Lots ob folks jest want deir beer,
    Votah, watch yore vote.

Some am wet and some am dry,
    Doan know which am best to try,
Dat's de way wid you and I.
    Votah, watch yore vote.

Seems lak folks doan eben care,
    Votah, watch yore vote;

And den dey find dat dey is where?
    Votah, watch yore vote.

Den dey has lots to say,
How come things to be dis way,
Lak de things are here today?
Votah, watch yore vote.

Some gits 'lected for de graf',
Votah, watch yore vote;

All we gits is ol' horselaf,
Votah, watch yore vote.

Vote jest lak you want to do,
Find out first jest who am who,
Vote for him and he gits through.
Votah, watch yore vote.

After Election

The election task is over now,
    'Twas quite a load to tote;
And Smith got all the yells and cheers,
    But Hoover got the vote.

The mob that followed Smith around,
    And cheered him for a clown;
Went to the polls and voted straight,
    And likewise turned him down.

It broke his heart, it set him back,
    He will not run again;
He walked his plank and broke it down,
    He made it very plain.

There's one thing that's certain now,
    Results just now denote;
The man who gets the cheering
    Doesn't always get the vote.

Lodgeman

I believe in joining every lodge,
    And do so when I can;
I guess you'd call me—pardon me,
    A "lodgical man."

Rebekas always interest me,
    In that I'm Counselor;
I'm president of others, too,
    A member of Ben Hur.

Yes, in the Eagle Lodge I scream,
    The Lions hear me growl;
At the Lamb's Club I can always blat,
    The Wolves just make me howl.

In the Moose Lodge, I'm the High Podunk,
    And here I often go;
There's one lodge where I don't belong,
    And that's the C.I.O.

The Camel Lodge don't interest me,
    Maybe it's too dry;
But I join up with all the boys,
    And manage to get by.

I've passed through all the chairs there are,
    In the B.P.O.E.;
But when I left the railroad,
    I dropped the B.R.T.

I'll put my name on Mason's list.
  And pretty soon I guess;
I'll try my luck in another lodge,
  The K & L of S.

I'm a Chopper in the Woodman Camp,
  Likewise the K of P;
I know you're thinking at this time,
  It's the gypsy in me.

But boy O boy, the meeting nights,
  Just keep me on the go;
My wife thinks me a crazy loon,
  But that don't make it so.

But when I die and lodges come
  To pay respect to me;
I'm wondering what they all will do—
  For what a crowd there'll be.

"Casey" Jones, the Immortal

Come all ye old timers if you want to hear
What became of "Casey"—the brave engineer
Who left us in a hurry and took the final jump,
When the engine he was driving got an awful bump.

Now "Casey" went to heaven—Pete met him at the gate
And said, "We're glad to see you if you are a little late
We want for you to carry on and railroad as of yore
And we're sure you will not be lonesome on the "Golden Shore."

    "Casey" Jones, surely was delighted
    "Casey" Jones, hunted far and near
    "Casey" Jones was very much contented
    For never did he ever find another engineer.

They gave him gold and silver to build the railroad train,
He worked with lots of helpers, he worked with might and main;
'Till at last he saw the finish of his brightest, fondest dream
For he finished up a model that didn't use steam.

St. Peter was delighted—had a smile upon his lip
As he climbed aboard the engine for the trial trip;
For "Casey" ran the engine and did it with a grin
And with all the cars crowded they went for a spin.

    "Casey" Jones, pulled the golden throttle,
    "Casey" Jones, ariding on the air,
    "Casey" Jones, tooted loud the whistle
    He didn't have to worry about the crossings there.

The scheme it was successful; they ran without a jar,
They visited the planets with not a thing to mar
Like smoke and cinders, grease and dirt like we have here;
"Casey" wore the garb of angels—the brave engineer.

They built a bridge of silver across the river Stix,
For the boat was old and leaky and they didn't want to fix
The boat to carry souls across the river any more,
So "Casey" pulls the passenger on the "Golden Shore."

>   "Casey" Jones, working for St. Peter,
>   "Casey" Jones, you can always bet,
>   "Casey" Jones is working there in glory,
>   He runs a golden engine and is running there yet.

Pap

Folks I know all call me Dad,
I don't mind that a bit;
My children said it long ago
And I am used to it.

But what I hate—it makes me mad,
For some confounded sap
To walk right up and stop and spit,
Then say, "How are you Pap?"

I know that chicken mites and lice,
Crawl through my smelly clothes;
I seldom cut my hair or beard,
But goodness only knows;

That don't excuse this worthless guy,
Who is himself a yap;
And give him right to stop and say,
"Well, how are you, Pap?"

Sometime, someday I will get mad,
At this fresh "Pappy" guy;
Then right away I'll use my fist
To pop him in the eye.

I much expect I will get "jugged,"
Then this Guy'll raise his cap
And yell as police lead me away,
        "Goodbye, so long, Pap."

Trusty

Matt Kimes is a "lifer" in jail,
Thought his health was a little too frail;
Sent out a plea,
And the governor, he
Let him out to go and hunt quail.

The governor gave him a gun,
And away went Matt on the run;
Some were amazed,
While others were dazed,
And said, "I'm a son-of-a-gun."

If I ever get in the "stir,"
A word meaning jail, I aver;
I'll put a plea,
In great misery,
To go and hunt quail as it were.

So here's to the "lifer" in jail,
Who gets a lot of "fan" mail;
Just say to some "dick,"
"I think I am sick,
I want to out and hunt quail."

There's a racket, a new one for fair,
A queer one to get some free air;
It carried right through,
As good rackets do,
'Twas very unique, I declare.

Relief

The front page now will get a rest,
    For Dillinger is dead;
And he deserved the fate he met,
    A price was on his head.

He had no chance—all well and good,
    What chances did he give?
He shot and robbed relentlessly,
    Did he deserve to live?

He winked at every law we had,
    He killed, then hid away
Just like a rat—and like a rat,
    He died the other day.

But "hero worship" will live on,
    His name linked up with "fame";
No, honest folk won't call it that,
    They have another name.

So, let's forget this Dillinger,
    And laud the honest men;
Who live to serve the best they can,
    And live to serve again.

Luck

I've always heard the saying—
    "The good Lord will provide";
But for seeing evidence,
    I've always been denied.

Yet I'm a firm believer now,
    It worked, and just like that;
I needed things, and one thing was
    A summer time straw hat.

I couldn't spare the cash to buy,
    And then, doggone my hide,
I kept repeating all the time—
    "The good Lord will provide."

He did it too, and did it well,
    I got my hat, a wow;
It didn't cost a copper cent,
    But, I will tell you how.

My wife and I were following
    A big black motor car,
When, lo behold, a hat flew out
    And landed with a jar.

The car went on, I jammed the brakes
 And stopped and "just like that,"
I climbed out on the boulevard
 And got myself a hat.

Now this is why I changed my mind,
 Just after that there ride;
I am a firm believer now—
 "The good Lord will provide."

Hot Stuff

A young lady—yes indescreet,
Went home one night in the sleet;
And lo and behold,
She said she was cold
But suffered the most with her feet.

So she heated an iron 'till red,
Then placed the darned thing in her bed;
It set things on fire
And worked up her ire
Imagine the things that she said.

Though she gets cold as the frogs,
Who spend the night out in the bogs;
She never will sleep
With an iron to keep
The bed warm to warm up her "dogs."

When Grandmother Sang

When my grandmother sang all her favorite old hymns,
    In a minor key, soft and so low;
I would sit in a corner all by myself,
    While she rocked in her chair, to and fro.

That was music to me in the days that are gone,
    When she sang in that soft, minor key;
And I wish that tonight I could hear her sweet voice
    Which was always sweet music to me.

When thinking sometimes, it seems only a day,
    How I looked forward with glee;
When she'd finish her work and take her big chair,
    And sing in that sweet minor key.

Her favorite position was facing the light,
 When the fireplace cast a deep glow;
There she'd rock and she'd sing in that quaint minor key
 And it was always soft and so low.

But now she is gone to that bright golden shore,
 And from all pain and care she is free;
But I know she sings in that sweet angel choir,
 And she'll sing in that sweet minor key.

To Ma

When all the folks have gone to bed,
When daily cares have all been shed,
My thoughts come out and run ahead,
    I'm thinking then of you.

Here in my chair I sit and smoke,
And even now I almost spoke
To you, but 'twas a joke.
    I'm thinking now of you.

For you are there and I am here,
You're far away and yet so near,
My drowsy eyes don't make it clear.
    I'm thinking always of you.

Together we have climbed the hill,
Though blustery winds near stopped us, still
We trudge along and always will.
    I'm thinking, so are you.

The Past is past. The future lies
Not far beyond, where earth and skies
Meet and guard a great surprise.
    I'm thinking, so are you.

When all are gone but you and me,
I hope that I shall ever be
Close in your thoughts, eternally.
    I'm thinking, then of you.

My Boy

I see our son's makin' speeches
    Tellin' all about the Press;
Gosh, how we would like to hear him,
    When he speaks about success.

'Taint so many years back yonder,
    When he was a little kid;
He laughed at Ma when she would lecture
    Which she very often did.

When I'd storm around about him
    Getting careless in his ways,
He never paid me much attention,
    Way back in the other days.

Ma and I have often wondered,
    How he'd make it later on;
All too soon he up and left us,
    First we knew it, he was gone.

Now we learn that he is talkin'
    Tellin' others what to do;
People go to hear him lecture,
    And we'd like to hear him, too.

Wonder now while he is talkin',
    If he thinks back now and then,
To the days away back yonder,
    Seems to hear his Ma again?

But, law me, what could we tell him
    How to live for great success;
Ma and me could not get started
    'Bout "Publicity and the press."

Yes we feel content to listen,
    Hear his logic, see his vim;
And we bet he's tellin' others
    Lots of things we told to him.

The Passing Flapper

Salutations, little girl,
    You have set our hearts awhirl
With your dainty rolled down socks,
    And your boy trimmed shingled locks.

Face the color none can tell,
    Painted often, painted well;
Dresses hitting at the knee,
    Giving legs more liberty.

Waists cut low in front, behind,
    The thinnest grade, the flimsy kind;
Skirts so scant and mighty tight,
    One sees through both day and night.

Silken stockings now and then
    Carry pictures of the men.
Yours the motor call at will
    Yours the pace that's set to kill;

Suppers at the midnight time,
    Fox trots to the tunes sublime.
Movies, sweets and boys galore,
    All are added to your store;

Living for the changing styles,
    Life is short but full of smiles.
Though the pace is very fast,
    Enjoy it then until at last

Paint and powder fail to hold
    That youthful look and now you're old.
Now "sign off" and just forget,
    Without a sigh, without regret;

You've lived your life, you've had your fling,
    Old age crept up and left his sting;
In after years just turn and smile,
    You're left behind a many a mile.

Abner

The wheels from his toys are scattered around,
   But gone is the fair little boy
Who played with his dumpcarts, cannons and tools,
   With heart bubbling over with joy.

Here on a visit, just for a day,
   But creeping close into our heart;
We miss him, the sunbeam, that's just what he is,
   And lonely we gaze at his cart.

Yes, mother and I are both growing old,
   But grandpa and grandma we'll be
To the fair little cherub, who loves us we know,
   And hope for a bright destiny.

His smile and his laughter still hover around
   We think he still must be here;
And sometimes we're hunting this fair little boy,
   Who's far away now, yet so near.

But he'll come again, this fair little boy,
   He'll find all his toys and things
Just where we put them to keep them for him
   We'll welcome the sunshine he brings.

Gene or Jean

They say you've named the baby, dear,
    The one you've never seen,
You took a chance and placed a bet
    And called the baby "Gene."

I'll say you're wise, both of you,
    In this name giving biz;
For if the boy should be a girl,
    Why, Jean it surely is.

For granddad just won't give a darn
    Be it girl of boy;
Just bring it home so Dad and Ma
    Can have it to enjoy.

We know right now, you know it too
    You now just what I mean
We'll love it well, and so will you
    Be it Gene or Jean.

Logic

My grandson came from school today,
    And shouts for all the town:
"I clumb the pole and retched right up
    And drug the derned thing down."

His rule for language was a "bust,"
    For once I did not care;
It did not jar me as it should,
    I saw his logic there.

He did the job and did it well,
    I gathered from his tale;
I've known of men who slumped and fell
    Tho' graduates of Yale.

Depression sits upon a pole,
    While we stand by and frown;
We've yet to see the man who "clumb"
    And "drug" the derned thing down.

We, all of us, are in reverse,
    There's sound of stripping gears;
And yet we stand and calmly wait,
    To realize our fears.

There is a man who "clumb" the pole,
    That's waiting for the call
To lead us out, as Moses did,
    Away from all the pall.

This man will glorify his name,
    Be he Jones of Brown;
He'll be the man who "clumb the pole,
    And drug the derned thing down."

                        Gene.

Ab the Yodeler

Ab has learned to yodel now,
    He yodels all the while;
He yodels in the plain old way
    And in the fancy style.

You hear him "a de laddie ooh,"
    When he gets out of bed,
All others say "Good morning, folks,"
    "Yo hoo" with him instead.

He starts with trash up to the hill,
    "A le a laddie ho—oo";
Then we listen when it comes,
    The echo "laddie o—o—o."

Sometimes the "laddie o—o—o"
    Garbles in his throat;
It's crossed between the puppies yelp
    And bleating of the goat.

"Ah le, ah la, a laddie ho,
    A le, ah la a le,
Ah le, a la a laddie o,"
    All the day sings he.

My Chauffeur

John, my little chauffeur boy,
    He runs the car all day;
And when at night he's tired out
    We put the car away.

He rounds the corners at full speed,
    The chickens have to fly;
For he hits her up a merry clip
    When he shifts her into high.

He drives her 'bout a thousand miles,
    Then gradually he stops;
Removes his cap and goggles,
    And out he quickly hops

To see if he has punctured
    A tire, or needs some oil;
And he examines everything
    From spark plug to the coil.

If everything just suits him
    He honks with might and main;
And shifts from first to second speed,
    Then into high again.

He drives her there and back again,
 And only stops to eat,
For he has some friends acomin'
 Whom he has to meet.

And at night when the gas is low,
 And engine parts are cold;
We tuck him in his trundle bed,
 For John is four years old.

The Hillbilly

You say yer drawin' pitchers and
    Would like fer me to sit
Still fer jest a minute while
    You up and finish it?

No, stranger, now yer money ain't
    No good to me at all;
I start with nothing in the spring
    And have less in the fall.

But you can draw me all yer like.
  And if you do not mind,
I'll tell you all jest where I live,
  It's easy like to find.

I live way down on Muddy Crick,
  You have to cross a bridge,
And take the trail right through the brush,
  To git to Rabbit Ridge.

You pass the Huskin' Corner by—
  They don't husk there no more,
'Cause corn ain't grown to husk, you know,
  The prices are too pore.

The next place on your right is mine,
  And it ain't much to see;
But it is there, you're welcome, too,
  Fer it is home to me.

Don't have to bother 'bout no gate,
  It fell down long ago;
The posts, they rotted plumb in two,
  And I jest left it so.

There is a barn, but it's no good,
  It's likely to upset;
'Twouldnt make no difference, cause
  There's nothing to get wet.

I had some critters—five or six,
    But they jest up and died;
I tried to sell, but had no luck,
    They wasn't worth their hide.

Then there's the hogs—jest two of them,
    But they are crackerjacks;
Some folks said, and jest fer fun,
    That they were razorbacks.

No one ever comes my way,
    The trail is orful rough;
And folks all ride, they do not like
    Much of this walkin' stuff.

Haint been to town for nigh' a year.
    Haint had no call to go;
Haint had no money fer to spend
    And no one there I know.

I never shave at all no more,
    My razor done got lost;
I kaint afford no other one,
    No matter what they cost.

I don't need much in way of clothes,
    Most anything will do
To kiver up my nakedness,
    And shed the wind off, too.

And thus I live, all by myself,
    I guess I kaint complain;
I'll let 'er rip and snort and buck,
    'till good times come again.

                 Gene.

Iowa

You can sing of old Montana
    And its climate, you say, "grand,"
Where the natives spend their money
    To meet you with a band;

And when you come they welcome you
    With open arms and say,
"This is Old Montana
    And we hope that you will stay."

Of course you have your scenery,
    It's been there quite awhile,
With us, who live in God's land,
    We have a change of style.

Your mountains stand just so each day,
    They never move nor sway;
They stand and watch, like sentinels,
    Your actions, by the way.

You do not sing of "Bad Lands"
    Or "twenty feet of snow,"
Or "prickly pear," or "cactus plant,"
    Or "fifty-eight below."

You sing of praises that you thought
    Were there on every hand;
Believe us, what you really saw
    Was Old Montana "sand."

Where is your grass and trees and such,
    That makes up half the show?
Now say, own up you miss them,
    That's what we want to know.

We half believe you're hypnotized,
    They've worked upon your eye,
In place of things you love the best,
    You just see "alkali."

The corn they're hauling here,
    As smooth as the banana,
Would cover up, just four feet deep
    The whole state of Montana.

It's hard to make the rhymes we want,
    It's hard to make them fit;
For this is good old IOWA,
    And we're might proud of it.

Spring Signs

When robins come to build their nests,
When all the song birds sing their best,
And the breeze is gentle, south of west,
    By these you know 'tis spring.

When pussy willows grow their fuzz,
When bees come round with well-known buzz,
And longs to sting, and sometimes does,
    By these you know 'tis spring.

When green things pop up from the ground,
And timid wild flowers can be found,
And bull frogs croak a joyful sound,
    By these you know 'tis spring.

When men look up their garden seeds,
And buys lot more than what he needs,
And plans to do some wondrous deeds,
    By them you know 'tis spring.

There are some signs that you can trust,
When other signs blow up or bust,
I count on then, I think I must,
    By them you know 'tis spring

Hey

Down the lake at a place I know
I'd like, just once more now, to go
And with the water smooth as glass,
"Still-fish" there for small-mouth bass.

I'd like to feel him pull again
When taking minnows hard, and then
I'd match my wits against his skill,
And reel him in against his will.

I've done all this, you bet 'twas fun
To watch the line when he would run
And jump and try to "throw" the bait,
Or break the line at any rate.

And so I say, I'd like to go
Down the lake to a place I know,
And with the water smooth as glass,
"Still-fish" there for small-mouth bass.

Longing

Did you ever have a longing, along about July,
To go once more a fishin', where we used to, you and I?
Of course we'd not be selfish, we couldn't be so rank,
As to even start a fishin' and not take Hank.

Old "Rocky Point's" a shoutin' and a hollerin' for fair
About the bass and channel-cat and pickerel that are there;
I seem to see old Henry catch a turtle now and then
And then my mind goes wandering back to the catfish—Big Ben.

And a fishin' there for minnows before 'tis hardly light,
For we felt that early minnows were the ones that got the bite;
We never called it working, we thought that it was play,
And it never seemed to tire us, we could go most every day.

And when the fishin' there was slow we'd leave it with a slam
And fish for carp and bull-heads, at a place above the dam;
For fishin' is just fishin', 'twas the sport for which we'd care
And old Henry could catch turtles there as well as anywhere.

While he held that darned umbrella between him and the sun
And cussed those slimy turtles, for he cussed them everyone;
And I'll be there if you will go, I'll meet you in July,
And we'll go once more a fishin', you and Hank and I.

We'll sit around the campfire and tell 'em of yore,
For you cannot tell a yarn too big to make the others sore;
And we'll live again those happy days, when you and I were boys,
For I've memories dear stored up inside of Sunny Illinois.

Hot

During all this sultry weather,
    It's a pretty common sight;
To watch the whole darn family,
    Find a place to sleep at night.

They wrestle with the mattress,
    And drag it here and there,
And try their best to locate,
    A place where there is air.

They first try out the sitting room,
    Then to the parlor go;
And think they've found a haven,
    And lie down in a row.

They sweat and toss about again,
    'Til someone will declare;
That they will "just be jiggered"
    If there's a breath of air.

Again they grab the mattress,
    And drag it as before;
They take it to another room,
    And place it on the floor.

And here they find it warmer yet,
    Again they move around;
And someone will speak up and say,
    "'Tis the warmest place we've found."

And thus it goes the whole night through,
    Until the morning light;
You find that you've been working,
    While you're resting in the night.

Autumn

'Tis autumn in the northern land,
    And all the trees and shrubs and such
Are flaunting out in full dress suits,
    Until you can't improve them much.

The maple and the oak are red,
    The pines a vivid green,
The birch and poplar, yellow mix
    In blending color scheme.

But all too soon they turn to brown,
    To fall and blow away,
Until the spring time calls to them
    To come another day.

Now soon old winter will appear,
    And winds will moan and sigh;
The leaves will wave you Au Revoir,
    They never say goodbye.

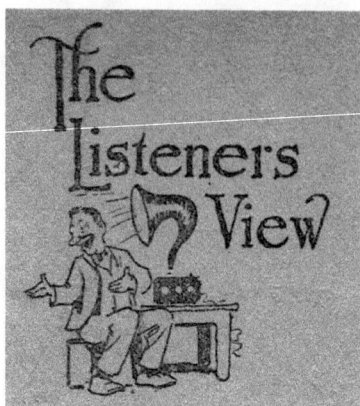

1925 Series Radio

We thank you for the service,
    You gave to us each day;
Broadcasting Base Ball classics
    We got it play by play.

It was just like being at the games,
    It came in loud and clear;
And when you said, "They're yelling,"
    We could almost hear them here.

And when 'twas cold in Washington,
    We shivered with the rest,
Although fifteen hundred miles away,
    Out in the Middle West.

Out seats were just like box-seats,
    More comfortable, I'd say,
We surely had it on the crowd –
    No one in our way.

We hollered, yelled and tore our hair
    When someone hit the ball,
And it soared both high and far away,
    Over the right field wall.

We saw them cheer "Old Barney,"
    Saw Coolidge toss the sphere;
And watched the band march 'round the field
    And thought we heard it here.

We saw the umpires working hard
    To watch and call them right;
We saw the wind blow piles of dust,
    We even saw the fight.

And when it rained the last grim day,
    We listened in, you bet
We felt a dozen times to see
    If we were getting wet.

We saw Cuyler make the smash,
    That settled all the show
We hear and saw all seven games,
    Hurrah for radio.

Fifty thousand paid each day
    But that's no crowd at all,
About two million "listened in"
    And hear and saw it all.

The Rampant "Pepper-Pod"

And now let's see this "Pepper-Pod,"
    John Martin is his name;
Who stood the A's right on their heads,
    And won undying fame.

He had the great Ruth's batting form,
    Tris Speaker's fielding eye.
He stole the bases right and left,
    Which put to shame "O'd Ty."

Three-in-one not one in three,
    They called him "dirty face";
But he showed the Athletic team
    How to steal a base.

What ho! This rookie, who is he
    To teach them all the way
Just how the game of ball is played
    That would save the day?

They tried to stop his wild parade,
    But gave up in despair;
When Mickey tried to head him off
    The "Pepper" wasn't there.

More power to him, this Martin boy,
    Who gave their tails a twist;
If he keeps up this mad career,
    His name will top the list

The Series o'er the Air

There's shouts of joy in old New York,
    And tears in Washington;
The Giants won four mighty games
    The "Nats," they just got one.

Some fifth thousand saw each game
    And watched the players play;
About ten million listened to
    The radio's relay.

Of course the crowd all took a hand,
    In managing the teams;
The managers themselves were bad,
    But capable, it seems.

The lame, the bland, the halt and sick,
    Set up a hue and cry;
When Bolton hit in place of Rice,
    The crowd all wondered why?

"How come they leave the pitcher in
    To throw the game away;
Can't Cronin figure otherwise?"
    The strategists all say.

They talk right back—a thousand miles,
    To him who was the "Mike";
They curse and swear and shake their fists
    Cut didoes and the like.

They have to get it off their chests
    They do—but just the same;
They have to rant and tear their hair,
    'Tis part of this great game.

Who'd care to go and see them play
    And never say a word?
No one, I venture here to say,
    'Twould really be absurd.

So let them shout and make their threats,
    And throw a fit or two;
They'll all be back a year from now,
    I'll sure be there—will you?

Another "Dizzy" Day

Well "Dizzy" pulled the Tiger's fangs
    You know, he said he would;
And everyone just wondered, now
    If "Dizzy" really could.

But "Dizzy" had no doubts at all
    He told them what he'd do;
You know that is a way with him
    He says it and it's true.

He'd pitch a ball game every day
    "No trouble, not at all";
But he is wise and leaves some games
    For his brother, Paul.

And thus St. Louis had a cinch,
    With Dean or Dean to pitch;
With "Diz" and "Daff" in brother act,
    They wouldn't have to switch.

One one day and one the next,
    Until the season ends;
What are they worth to baseballdom?
    Well now that depends.

Those Dean guys sure do have the stuff,
    Believe it now or not;
They licked all teams within the league,
    And proved that they were "Hot."

Jerome ties knots in Tigers' tails
    He did it fair and square
He pitched and beat them yesterday
    And had a lot to spare.

If "Diz" can beat this Tiger bunch
    What will "Daffy" do?
If history does repeat itself,
    "Daff" will follow through.

The Second Game

The second game was quite a show
    St. Louis lost to Schoolboy Rowe:
There are some folks who thought, I ween,
    No one could pitch but "Dizzy" Dean.

Twelve innings "Schoolboy" turned them back
    And then "Goose" gave the ball a crack,
That closed the gate for Thursday's show,
    Chalk up a game for Schoolboy Rowe.

Rowe, a pitcher tall and lean,
    Is different from this "Dizzy" Dean,
Who blows his horn both long and loud
    And struts his stuff before a crowd.

It takes all types to play the game.
    No matter what's the player's name
There's others in the game, you know
    Besides this Dean and Schoolboy Rowe.

The fielders who with watchful eyes,
    Pull down the balls that hit the skies,
The basemen are not there for fun
    The batters who knock in the run

All play their part in the great game,
    And help the pitchers on to fame
All of which goes on to show
    All can't be Deans nor Schoolboy Rowe.

Tigers Go Daffy

The Tigers fled in wild dismay,
 The Deans got loose again;
The Tigers ran for cover for
 They remember when

The Deans go on a rampage
 There's nothing else to do
But get into their dug-out
 And hide themselves from view.

The third game they were helpless,
 Before this "Daffy" Dean;
Both "Diz" and "Daf" now have a game,
 The family's record clean.

Detroit fans went crazy
 When the games were even, all;
St. Louis wasn't bothered much—
 They hadn't pitched their "Paul."

But now he's tucked away his game,
 It's time for them to shout;
For "Dizzy" says he'll pitch again,
 And promises a rout.

So far the Dean boys have it,
    And no one can say "No";
They drove the Tigers to their lair
    And made them lay down low.

Will "Dizzy" win the fourth ball game,
    And will they win them all?
"Dizzy" says they'll turn the trick
    And so does brother Paul.

Bridges Beats the Dean

Yes, Bridges crossed the Rubicon,
    He beat the "Dizzy" Dean
Who bragged about just what he'd do;
    You all know what I mean.

Now "Dizzy" didn't even say
    That belt upon his bean
Was his undoing yesterday,
    And slowed up "Dizzy" Dean.

No alibi, I haste to say,
    Would do him any good;
He said he'd beat them anyway,
    And really thought he could.

But Bridges had another thought,
    He pitched a master game;
And never wavered 'til he knew
    Those "Cards" were really tame.

Detroit, now is out in front
    With Schoolboy Rowe on hand;
And if he wins Detroit folks
    Will yell, "Strike up the Band."

The Cards will pitch another Dean,
    "Dizzy's" brother, Paul;
They cannot chance the other boys,
    For they have tried them all.

Carleton failed while Vance fell down,
    Walker tried and tried;
Then Haines and Mooney flung a while
    But they too stepped aside.

So now it's up to "Daffy" Dean
    To even up the score;
And if he really turns the trick,
    They'll have to play some more.

Finis

The last game was a riot,
    St. Louis–son'a guns,
Wouldn't let the Tigers score,
    While they got eleven runs.

The Tigers gave them all they had
    St Louis took it all;
They hogged it from the very start
    And won a game of ball.

That makes St. Louis champions
    In nineteen thirty-four;
And when the last man made an out,
    Up went an awful roar.

The game was marred by irate fans,
    Who took the game in hand;
And banished "Ducky" Medwick from
    The St Louis band.

They claimed he played some dirty ball,
    And would not let him play;
The game was stopped for half an hour,
    The fans just had their way.

The classic now is history
    For nineteen thirty-four;
Next year the winning teams
    Will meet and play some more.

Homecoming

This morn I wakened early, why, I couldn't even think,
And for a time I wondered, my eyes would only blink;
'Twas then I just remembered and heard somebody say,
"Get up and get agoin', children's comin' home today."

And then I knew 'twas Christmas, and I sprang up like a shot,
They'd be here before we knew it and just as like as not
We'd not be ready for 'em, after plannin' every way,
And my, it's excitin', children's comin' home today.

Ma goes 'round a lookin', what for I don't know,
She gives me jolly thunder because I am so slow;
I say, "What is the hurry," and then she'd up and say,
"You seem to be forgettin' children's comin' home today.

And then they come in laughin',
right glad that they are here,
For this is what they've waited for and waited for a year;
And Ma and I are happy and have a lot to say,
The thing that made us happy is, the children came today.

Gene

Thanksgiving Day

Dad Says:

> "There comes a day and soon, by gum,
> When all our friends will gladly come
> To see how much we'll have to eat,
> And if there'll be an extra seat
> For just one more and they will find,
> This day is made for just their kind."

Ma Says:

> "My gracious me, how short the time
> To get the things, I'll bet a dime
> I can't get anything I want
> And everyone is looking gaunt;
> I never will have anything
> That's fit to eat, like others bring."

We all say:

> "By jimminee, this is the day
> We eat to live, so eat away;
> Such food at this won't make us sick,
> So fill the platters high and quick.
> Remember this, where e'er we stay,
> We're welcome here Thanksgiving Day.

The Day After

Full of turkey, pie and stuff,
I had more than just enough;
Ate until I thought I'd bust,
Nothin' left but bones and crust.

Funny what a man will do,
Can't quit eatin' when he's through;
Eats as long as it's in sight,
Next day feels just like a fright.

Glad these meals don't come each day,
If they did old "Heck" would pay;
No wonder people have the gout,
And ponder what it's all about.

Still this day was made to eat,
Give your stomach, then, a treat;
Then give thanks and likewise pray,
That you're alive and well today.

Near Christmas

Have you noticed how your son has changed,
    He jumps when you first call
And does the work and does it well,
    That he wouldn't do at all
At any other season, take the whole year through;

    I know just what the matter is
    And so I guess, do you.

Have you noticed how your daughter does
    Just as she's told to do,
And hustles 'round and makes the bed,
    And washes dishes, too
Without a word or grumble, without a fret or stew,

    I know just what the matter is,
    And so I guess, do you.

Have you noticed how when father dear
    Comes from his work at night,
And mother runs and waves her hand
    When first he comes in sight;
She walks with him clear in the house,
    And supper's ready, too,
    I know just what the matter is
    And so I guess, do you.

Have you noticed, friend, when mother wants
    The bucket filled with cobs,
That father sees her first of all,
    And rushing out, he robs
The others of the pleasure, and gets the water too,

        I know just what the matter is,
            And so I guess, do you.

Have you noticed how the time has flown,
    Since you've noticed this before?
It won't be long 'till Santa Claus
    Is knocking at your door;
And everybody's doing just the best that he can do;

        I know just what the matter is,
            And so I'll bet, do you.

Christmas

'Tis getting 'bout the time of year
When all the old folks want to hear
That all the kids from far and near
    Are coming home for Christmas.

And mother smiles and nods her head,
While letters from the young folks said,
"All other plans are off, instead
    We're coming home for Christmas."

The mother dear begins to plan
In just the way that mothers can
To entertain the joyous clan
    That's coming home for Christmas.

And Dad, he slyly steps around,
He tells no one just what he's found,
But covers just a lot of ground
    For those who come for Christmas.

Bob brings his family, rather small
He drives right up and one and all
Rush out to greet and hear him call
    "Well, here we are for Christmas."

And Margaret comes with both her boys,
With no apology for noise,
For this is one of many joys –
    To be at home for Christmas.

And thus they come 'till all are there,
They come in from "the land knows where,"
And drive away all thoughts of care,
    For they've come home for Christmas.

A Punk Santa Claus

Suppose we'd dress old Santa Claus
    As the men dress up today;
And shave his beard, and cut his hair,
    What would the children say?

If he appeared in full dress suit,
    With shoes the latest style,
And high silk hat and white necktie,
    Without that sunny smile;

But had a walking stick with him,
    And he was tall and thin;
And came right up to your front door,
    Would children let him in?

Supposed he told them who he was,
    Would they be satisfied?
Or would they think he'd "bunkoed" them,
    And "humbugged" them besides?

Would he be then the same old man,
    We see from year to year?
He couldn't change the smallest mite
    And fool us, never fear.

Oh, no, we'll leave him as he is.
 Just plump and fat and gay;
So watch him when he appears,
 He comes on Christmas Day.

He'll leave his pack chucked full of toys,
 His sleigh and reindeer, too;
His fur trimmed suit, his jaunty cap,
 I'll know him then, will you?

Ford and Cadillac

When riding in your brand new Ford,
    All shining bright with paint;
Don't think you're in a Cadillac,
    For you know darned well you ain't.

All others know the self same fact,
    It's useless to pretend;
It works just fine for quite a while,
    But not so in the end.

Some folks look what they are not,
    And make believe they are;
They sail along for quite a while,
    But don't get very far.

So be yourself and play the game
    Watch out how you pretend;
I'd rather look just what I am,
    Than foolish in the end.

And so, when riding in your Ford,
    Don't have too stiff a back;
'Cause people know the difference 'twixt,
    The Ford and Cadillac.

Do It Now

There is no yesterday, my dear,
    There may be no tomorrow;
So spread the golden sunshine now,
    And drive away all sorrow.

The time is all to short, my dear,
    To always be fault finding;
So try and cheer the doubting ones,
    Their queerness never minding.

There is no yesterday, my dear,
    There may be no tomorrow;
Your chances pass before you know,
    You'll learn it then in sorrow.

When Day is Done

The day is done; but count it won,
If thou, some kindly deed hath done
To start a smile upon its way,
An endless journey day by day,
   Ere day is done.

The day is done, but do not sleep
If thou has caused someone to weep
By thoughtless deed, until you right
The wrong before 'tis night,
   Then day is done.

The day is done; let peace and joy
And happiness without alloy
Be yours to hold within your hand,
While standing in the promised land
   When day is done.

The Battler

Here comes "Old Tige," an alley cat.
    A yellow streak of brawn
A homlier cat, or a wiser cat,
    None have looked upon.

His ears chewed off, his head all swelled
    He slinks along with grace;
He fears no one nor anything,
    Friendly? — not a trace.

He has no friends, he hates them all,
    And everyone hates him;
He plays the game, but plays alone,
    He plays it with a vim.

He sneaks with belly near the ground,
    And looks straight on—afar;
But sees it all what e're goes on,
    Knows what his chances are.

He's no one's pet and has no home,
    Yet he is slick and trim;
He gives no quarter, asks for none,
    My hat is off to him

So here's to "Tige," the alley cat,
    A toast to him with wine;
There's no deception in his life,
    Like that in yours and mine.

Quiet, Please

'Tis not the mule with the loudest bray,
    That pulls the hardest on the dray;
'Tis not the man with the pouter chest,
    Who does more work than all the rest.

There's a bit of action back behind,
    And at this place you'll always find
'Tis not the noise that makes the show,
    But quiet ones who act, you know.

But mules will bray and men will strut,
    They never shove us from the rut;
So thank the Lord and thank Him strong
    We have the quiet force along.

Man Wants Little Here Below

If I cannot have the whole blamed earth,
    Then give me just a slice;
Construct a fence around it
    And fix the thing up nice.

And please put up a modern house,
    With taxes—never due,
And pave the way clear round the place
    I leave it up to you.

And then put up a big garage
    To hold my motor car
That runs me down on "Easy Street"
    Without the slightest jar,

And put me down at my club door,
    Where assessments have been paid;
And there I'll meet my many friends
    Who, too, their pile have made.

Cut out the cost it takes to live,
    With goods sent, send receipt;
I hope I'm not monotonous
    Or do not show conceit.

Give me a "roll" to flash around
    In sight of all my friends;
Then let me live a good long time,
    For Death, the whole thing ends.

And then "The Reaper" calls on me,
    There'll be no pockets in my shirt
That I will wear when going out
    To die and turn to dirt.

If I cannot have the whole blamed earth,
    And you, these things can give;
I'll doff my hat in thanks to you,
    And I'll proceed to live.

Faith

Your faith in me will grow and grow
Until some other day
You'll read some rhyming you will not like
It'll wither then away.

Hope

Lives of great men oft remind us
That great we might be if we try
And although I'm not pathetic
Perhaps I will be by and by.

Charity

The alms we give are not in vain
Like bread cast on the sea
So try your hand at casting some
Mayhap it comes to me.

My Mother's Faith

If I could have my mother's faith
    In God's Eternity,
I know I would not be afraid
    Twould be all right with me.

She stands upon the brink today,
    Her eyes uplift in prayer;
She knows she will her Master see
    And find him waiting there.

And when it comes my time to cross
    The Bar, O let me be
Bathed in the faith my mother had
    Of God's Eternity.

The Long, Long Trail

I heard of a trail, "The long, long trail,"
 With a one way blaze you can see;
And as near as I know, and I've wondered a lot,
 This trail is the one, then, for me.

I have never seen one who has been and come back,
 To tell where it led to and why;
I am anxious to know where it took them all to,
 And these things I will know bye and bye.

They must be contented–it's always the same–
 Not a line back do they send;
They wave you goodbye and snap out their light,
 And pass out of sight round the bend.

There's lots of them travel this "long, long trail,"
 Millionaires, derelicts and such;
The poor ones, the rich ones, the happy and sad,
 They say that it matters not much.

Those that are tired, worn out with this life,
 Who seeking the haven of rest;
Will look and then ponder and then after all
 They pick out the "Long Trail" as best.

I've looked up the markings, they say it is plain,
 With the one way blaze on the tree;
And when I am feeling just right for the trip,
 'Twill be the "long trail" then, for me.

Passing

How sweet to die as one would choose,
And thus the passing then would lose,
The sting of death, the pain, the fear
For loved ones left behind one here.

How sweet to go as one would please,
Among beloved orange trees
That one himself had planted there,
And tended with loving care.

How sweet a memory left behind,
That, searching, one may always find
The good one did from day to day
Will be his monument for aye.

What Then

When I have lived my term of years,
And turn to dust again;
I wonder what's in store for me,
I wonder now, what then?

I roam in fields of fancy free,
But in the great Amen;
No man can tell me anything
Of when I'm gone. What then?

Over the Hill

It's only a little way over the hill,
    Beyond the shadow line;
A trip that many a foot has trod,
    A trip that soon is mine.

Over the hill I'll meet my friends
    That have gone on before;
I'm weary, tired, ready to go,
    After my own four score.

The long black shadows slowly creep
    Close to the bed where I lie;
As if to hide what I shall see,
    After I say "Goodbye."

I'm not afraid to start alone,
    Be it night or day;
For well I know the Master will
    Meet me and point the way.

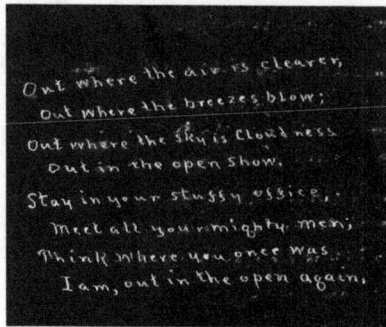

Untitled

Out where the air is cleaner,
 Out where the breezes blow;
Out where the sky is cloudless
 Out in the open show.

Stay in your stuffy office,
 Meet all your migty men;
Think where you once was
 I am out in the open again

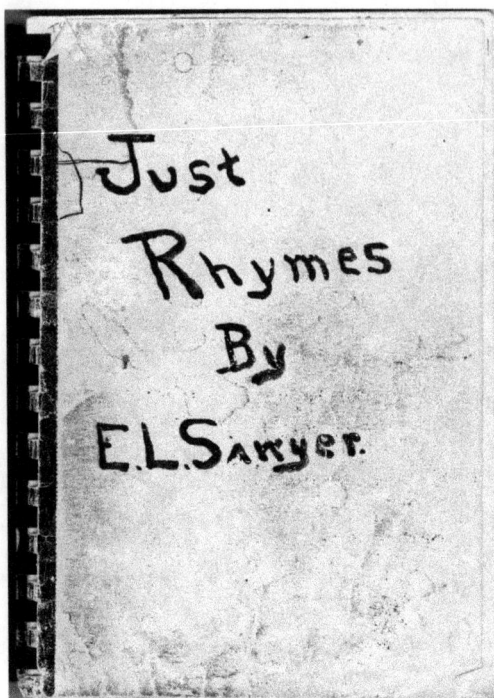

Just
Rhymes
By
E.L.Sawyer.

Notes on Poems

The Zepher:

In the depths of the depression a new train was invented to invigorate declining rail travel. The Pioneer Zephyr was a diesel-powered, high-speed, streamlined stainless steel train that was far ahead of its time. It ran from Chicago throughout the Midwest to Denver. E. L. probably saw the Zephyr in Kansas City.

The Zeppelin:

For more than nine years two German rigid airships, the *Hindenburg* and the *Graf Zeppelin* carried mail and passengers across the Atlantic. This came to an end on May 6. 1937 when the *Hindenburg* crashed and burned in New Jersey.

Edison:

This poem was sent to the Edison family and is believed to be in the Edison Museum in West Orange, New Jersey. There is a note from the family thanking E. L. for the poem.

The word "aye" used in the third stanza is pronounced "ay" and means always or forever.

Lindbergh:

Lindbergh crossed the Atlantic on May 20-21, 1927. E. L. likely heard the radio broadcast of his landing and wrote this poem shortly thereafter. You can listen to the broadcast of Lindbergh's arrival, perhaps the very same one listened to by E. L., at http://charleslindbergh.com.

All Will be Well:

Will Rogers, the great American humorist and social commentator was killed on August 15, 1935 in a plane crash near Fairbanks, Alaska; his friend, Wiley Post who piloted the plane also died. Rogers was a friend of Lindbergh and was greatly admired by E. L.

"three points down" refers to all three wheels of an airplane on the ground.

Cocoanut:

In the spring of 1928 George White built a pedal-powered, wing-flapping ornithopter, in which he attempted to become airborne on the beach at St. Augustine, Florida. E. L. visited his brother Frank at Coco Beach, in 1926 and may have heard of this odd inventor.

Darius Green was the boy hero of an 1869 poem by John Townsend Trowbridge in which the aviation pioneer flapped his wings and fell flat. You can read the entire poem at http://www.skygod.com/quotes/darius.html

After Election:

The election of 1928 was between Republican Herbert Hoover and Democrat, Al Smith. The rumor was that if Smith, a Catholic was elected, the Pope would rule America from his own fortress in Washington, D.C. There were boisterous rallies for Smith in Iowa, but he lost to Hoover by twenty one percent.

Lodgeman:

"Rebekas" is the International Order of Rebekah Assemblies, a branch of the Odd Fellows (IOOF). Ben Hur Lodge is a Masonic organization and the Eagles are The Fraternal Order of Eagles (FOE), which was originally founded by those of the theatrical persuasion. Another theatrical organization, the Lamb's Club was named for the writer, Charles Lamb rather than the four-legged wool bearer. E. L. claimed to be the High Podunk of Moose Lodge, but Franklin Roosevelt and Harry Truman were actual members of the Loyal Order of Moose, and I would imagine, rather higher Podunks than he. When E. L. wrote that he doesn't belong to the CIO he is referring to the Congress of Industrial Organization which, headed by John L. Louis, fought bitterly in the mid 1930s with its parent, the AFL, the American Federation of Labor. The camel was the mascot of the Prohibition Party and thus necessarily dry. BPOE is the Benevolent and Protective Order of Elks; BRT the Brotherhood of Railroad Trainmen; K & L of S is Knights and Ladies of Security, which became the Security and Benefit Association and later an insurance company, and the K of P is the Knights of Pythias. E. L. claimed to be a "chopper in the Woodman Camp," which is the Woodmen of the World; their gravestones resemble stumps.

Casey Jones:

The story goes that Casey was making up time when he came upon a freight train stopped on his track. After telling his fireman to jump, he stayed with the engine and slowed it down to the point that he was the only one killed in the collision.

The Ballad of Casey Jones written in 1909 celebrates his bravery. However, another Casey Jones song from 1912 written by Joe Hill presents Casey as an anti-union worker who scabs for striking angels in heaven.

Pap:

Webster's New World Dictionary defines "pap" as a mash, paste or soft food for infants, oversimplified or tasteless writing or political graft.

Trusty:

The story of Matthew Kimes is true. The convicted murderer was serving a life sentence when he was let out to go quail hunting in November of 1934; he returned to prison after his jaunt. He was given another leave in 1945, but this time he chose to escape and rob a bank. While a fugitive, he was run over by a poultry truck and returned to prison but soon succumbed to his injuries.

Relief:

The gangster and bank robber, John Dillinger was killed in Chicago on July 22, 1934 as he exited a movie theater. As the first "Public Enemy Number One," he was the most famous of the Depression era mobsters. While his body lay on display in the Chicago morgue, more than 15,000 people viewed his bullet-riddled corpse.

When Grandmother Sang:

E. L.'s grandmother on his father's side was Sally C. Sandborn. She was born February 6, 1819 in Corinth, Vermont and married Dana M. Sawyer, also of Corinth on June 24, 1840. E. L.'s father, Henry P Sawyer, was born June 22, 1841. Sally Sawyer was our great-great-great grandmother.

To Ma:

E. L.'s mother, Sara Elizabeth Joiner was born November 2, 1842 in Wabash Indiana, and died in Creston on June 6, 1929. She was our great-great-grandmother.

My Boy:

E. L.'s son, Robert Lucas Sawyer, known to us "kids" as Uncle Bob Sawyer, was the editor of the *Trenton Republican Times* newspaper from 1928 until 1935.

The Passing Flapper:

Our grandmother, Margaret "Maggie" Sawyer Gantt was E. L.'s daughter. This poem was probably written about her when she was a rebellious teenager, in the late 1910s. By 1920 she was married and the mother of my father.

Abner:

Sally's father, my uncle and E. L.'s grandson, Franklin Abner Gantt.

Gene or Jean:

This poem was written in a letter dated October 12, 1920 to Maggie and her husband, Robert Fulton Gantt, known to us as Grandpa Butch. Maggie was pregnant with my father, Robert Eugene Gantt at the time, but they did not know if it would be a boy or a girl.

Logic:

Written about my father as an allegory to the Depression.

Ab the Yodeler:

About Franklin Abner Gantt, Sally's father.

My Chauffeur:
There are very few stories that any of us can remember about Grandpa Sawyer but I do recall my father telling me that he first learned to drive in an 1896 Oldsmobile, a motorized buggy with a tiller rather than a steering wheel, on Grandpa Sawyer's farm in Missouri.

A hand written note on the page from my uncle Ab says that this poem was inspired by my father, R. E. "Gene" Gantt

The Hillbilly:
Written about the cabin that E. L. and his wife Hannah had on U. S. 65 about 5 miles south of Trenton, Missouri. Perhaps a bit of an exaggeration.

Longing:
There is a Rocky Point Club on the Mississippi River in Quincy, Illinois, about 100 miles due east of Treton.

Hot:
In the sultry summer the Gantt family would visit E. L. and Frankie at their place on Highway 65 south of Trenton.

1925 Series Radio:
The first World Series to be broadcast on radio was the 1921 contest between two New York teams, the Yankees and the Giants. Although it was broadcast "live" the commentators were not at the game, but called the action based on reports they received via telegraph. By 1925 baseball on the radio was an established tradition.

The Pittsburgh Pirates played the Washington Senators, also known as the nationals or Nats. "Old Barney" was Barney Dryfuss, owner of the Pirates. Pittsburgh won the series when in the ninth inning of the seventh game, Kiki Cuyler hit a home run. It was so foggy that the umpires could not truly tell if the ball fell fair or foul.

The Rampant "Pepper Pod":

In the 1931 World Series, E. L. was enamored with John "Pepper" Martin, the St. Louis Cardinals rookie outfielder and third baseman. With an amazing performance by Martin, the Cardinals beat the Philadelphia Athletics in seven games. This poem was published in the *Trenton Republican Times* while E. L.'s son, Bob Sawyer was editor.

Tris Speaker, the "Grey Eagle," played from 1907 to 1928. He still holds the career record for doubles (792) and for the most double plays for an outfielder. "O'd Ty" refers to Ty Cobb who played 22 seasons with the Detroit Tigers. His record of stolen bases stood for 49 years.

The Series o'er the Air:

The 1933 World Series was between the New York Giants and the Washington "Nats." In the eleventh inning of game 4, Washington manager, Joe Cronin chose Chris Bolton to pinch hit instead of Sam Rice and Bolton hit into a double play to end the game. The Giants went on to win the series in five games.

"Cut didoes" means behaving in a silly or mischievous way.

Another Dizzy Day:

The next five poems are about the 1934 World Series between the St. Louis Cardinals and the Detroit Tigers. They were all published in the *Trenton Republican Journal*. Poems about games four and six are missing.

As the story goes, Jay Hanna Dean was nicknamed "Dizzy" because of his wild antics when he was a seventeen-year-old soldier. During the Depression years he was one of Baseball's major stars, the other being Babe Ruth. In the 1934 regular season Dizzy bragged that he and his brother Paul, "Daffy," would together win 45 games, and so they did. "If ya done it, it ain't braggin'."

The Second Game:

Lynwood Thomas Rowe, the second game pitcher for the Detroit Tigers, got the nickname "Schoolboy" when pitching as a teenager in a semi-pro baseball league and beating men twice his age. In 1934 he pitched twenty-one complete games, winning nineteen of them.

"Goose" Goslin drove in the winning run in the bottom of the twelfth inning. "Schoolboy" Rowe had pitched the entire twelve innings, but lost the game.

Tigers Go Daffy:

"Dizzy" Dean's brother was called "Daffy" mostly because the names sounded so good together in radio broadcasts. In many ways he was the opposite of his boisterous brother, but both were great pitchers. Between the two of them, they pitched five of the seven games and won two apiece.

Bridges Beats Dean:

In Game 5, Detroit pitcher Tommy Bridges outlasted "Dizzy" Dean to beat the Cardinals 3-1. Both pitched eight innings, but Dean was relieved in the ninth. Times were different back then. In the 1934 season, Bridges pitched 23 complete games and won 22 of them; now a complete game is a rarity. Unfortunately for St. Louis, "Dizzy" Dean's public prediction of victory failed to come true.

Finis:

Although it would be his fifth start in twelve days, "Dizzy" Dean insisted on pitching the final game of the World Series. He shut out the Tigers in a complete game while the Cardinals scored eleven runs. In the sixth inning, with St. Louis leading 7-0, Joe "Ducky" Medwick slid aggressively into third with a triple, upending Marv Owen and causing a row. The next inning, when Medwick took the field, he was pelted with anything the fans could throw at him. Even when the field was cleaned, the Detroit fans kept littering it in their ire. Eventually "Ducky" was removed from the game for his own safety.

Homecoming:
The photo at the beginning of this section shows E. L. and his wife, Frankie Hanna Sawyer in front of their cabin in Trenton. The poem is about a visit from family: Uncle Bob Sawyer "R. L.," Maggie and her husband, Robert Fulton Gantt "grandpa Butch," my dad, Gene and Sally's dad, Ab.

Christmas:
I think these two Christmas poems and the two Thanksgiving poems were written in the mid 1930s in the depth of the Depression.

Ford and Cadillac:
Written as a scold by E. L. to his son, Robert Lucas Sawyer.

Man Wants Little Here Below:
I think E. L. and Frankie were poor a good part of their life, especially their later years, and E. L. is praying to God to make him rich for just a little while.

My Mother's Faith:
E. L.'s mother, Sarah Elizabeth Joiner, was a schoolteacher in Creston Iowa for thirty years and was very much beloved by the community. When she left Creston in 1921, she was given a testimonial and $100 in gold, worth twelve times as much today. She died in 1929.

Over the Hill:
I don't now when E. L. died, but it seems that these four poems were written in his last days. He says he is "weary, tired, ready to go, after my own four score" which would indicate he died around 1954.

Untitled:
This brief rhyme is from a canvas-bound scrapbook and may have been hand-written by E. L. himself.

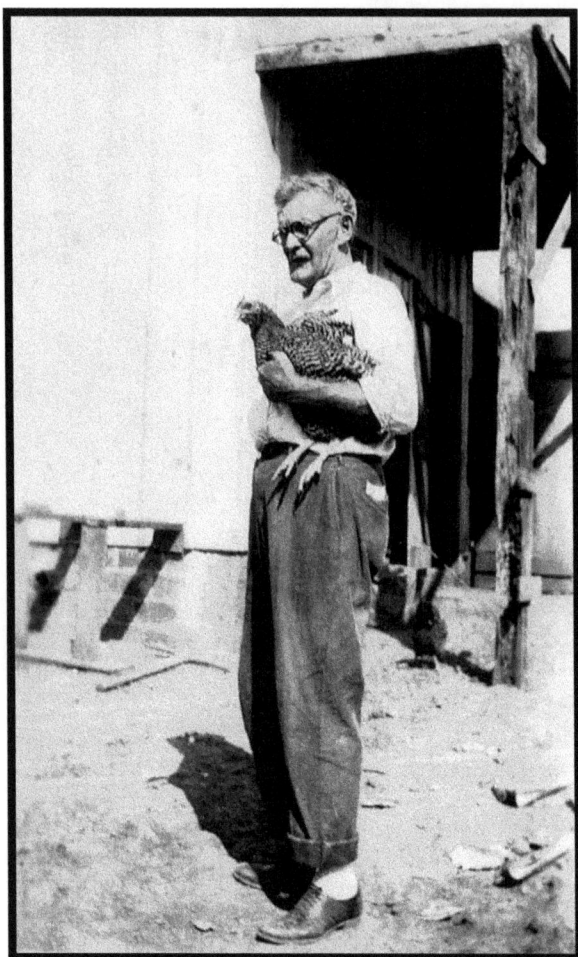

www.ingramcontent.com/pod-product-compliance
Lightning Source LLC
Chambersburg PA
CBHW050731030426
42336CB00012B/1508